AF317003

An Adoption Journal
and Memory Book

My Story: An Adoption Journal and Memory Book
Copyright © 2025 by Dayna Royston

Author website: https://authordaynaroyston.my.canva.site/

Printed in the United States of America
First Edition, 2025

A Note from the Author:

I created this memory book journal as a resource for children adopted after time in foster care. Adoptive parents and children can complete the pages together: adding photos, drawing pictures, and writing down thoughts as adoptees process their unique life stories. I have included different sections for journaling about first family, forever family, important events, memories, questions, and more. Each section ends with a space for reflection on a passage from Psalm 139. I pray that this memory book journal will promote healing and growth and become a treasured keepsake for years to come.

— *Dayna Royston*

this story belongs to:

You saw me before I was born. Every day of my life was recorded in your book. Every moment was laid out before a single day had passed. Psalm 139:16

FOR PARENTS AND CAREGIVERS: HOW TO USE THIS BOOK

This memory book journal is meant to be a special keepsake as well as a resource for supporting adoptive children as they discover and process their stories. Use this book to initiate important conversations, and add to it over time as the conversations continue. Spend personal, one-on-one time with your adopted child working on the pages together. Your child can attach photos, draw pictures, or write out details about themselves, their biological family, their adoptive family, and important events. The pages do not need to be completed in order. Some pages are left blank to be customized to your child's unique story. Encourage creativity to make this book reflect his or her personality and interests. Add scripture verses, songs, poems, awards, notes or cards from friends and family, etc. Most of all, plan times for your adopted child to be able to ask questions, share feelings, and find meaning and hope by embracing truths from God's Word.

FOR ADOPTEES: IDEAS FOR TELLING YOUR STORY

A Brief Description of the Sections in this Memory Book

MY TIMELINE
Starting with your birth year, write the years in the colorful arrows, then add specific dates and descriptions in the white tags. Include events such as your birthday, first day of school, time in foster care, adoption day, achievements, trips, or any other important dates in your life story.

THIS IS ME
Add a baby photo, school picture, or draw a self-portrait. List facts about when and where you were born, your ethnicity, and other details you want to include about the beginning of your story.

MY FAVORITES
Describe yourself by listing your favorite things. Color the crayon with your favorite color. Draw your favorite foods and animals or cut pictures out of magazines and glue them into your book. Add photos of you doing some of your favorite activities. Add more photos or journal your thoughts on the blank pages provided.

MY FIRST FAMILY
Attach photos, draw pictures, or write descriptions of your biological family. List facts and record special memories. It's o.k. to include sad or difficult memories as well. Even if you have limited information, you can still journal a letter and a prayer for your first family. Use the blank pages to journal, draw, add more photos, or write out poems or scripture.

MY JOURNEY
Tell the story of the time between your birth and your adoption. Did you live in different homes? Were there special people in your life, such as social workers, CASAs, pastors, counselors, or foster parents? Record memories and events from this part of your story. In the blank pages, add more about your journey such as awards, artwork, or notes from special people.

MY ADOPTION DAY
Write down your memories of your adoption day, add photos from the court hearing or adoption celebration, or draw pictures of the events of the day. You can use the "Encouraging Notes and Quotes" section for adoption party guests to leave a note of encouragement, or you can print out comments from social media or write out favorite quotes or Bible verses. If you will be leaving the book out for party guests to sign, you might want to wait to add personal information to the rest of the book *after* the party (for your privacy). Attach cards or additional photos to the blank pages.

MY FOREVER FAMILY
Add photos, drawings, or write out descriptions of your adoptive family. Record some favorite memories and activities. Attach photos of family time or vacations in the blank pages, journal about what makes your family unique, or write out a favorite song.

MY THOUGHTS
Take some time to think about your story. What questions do you have? What emotions do you feel? List some thoughts, and then journal in more detail on the blank pages. Talk through these questions and emotions with parents and counselors, tell God about how you feel, and write down comforting scripture verses.

MY DREAMS FOR THE FUTURE
Journal your plans and hopes for the future. Make some goals, then pray for God's guidance and direction as you follow His path and yield to His plans.

MY JOURNAL
Each section ends with a passage from Psalm 139. Read the verses, then answer the questions as you consider how those verses apply to you and your story.

CAN I TRUST GOD?
Learn about who God is and how you can know for sure that He is trustworthy.

HOW DO I BECOME GOD'S CHILD?
Read what the book of Romans says about how to live forever with God.

My timeline

JOURNAL

this is me!
my name
facts about me
my birthday

where I was born
More about me:

My favorites
Favorite Bible Verse
FAVORITE ANIMAL
favorite foods
favorite songs:
favorite color

Attach a photo here.
Doing what I love!
SPECIAL ABILITIES
Things I like to do:
Places I like to go:
Attach a photo here.
fun times!
Games I like to play:

O LORD. you have examined my heart
and know everything about me.
You know when I sit down or stand up.
You know my thoughts
even when I'm far away...
You know what I am going to say
even before I say it. LORD...
Such knowledge is too wonderful for me,
too great for me to understand!
Psalm 139:1-2. 4.6

 My JOURNAL

Do you ever feel invisible or misunderstood? God sees you, knows everything about you, **and He loves you!** How can that thought encourage your heart today?

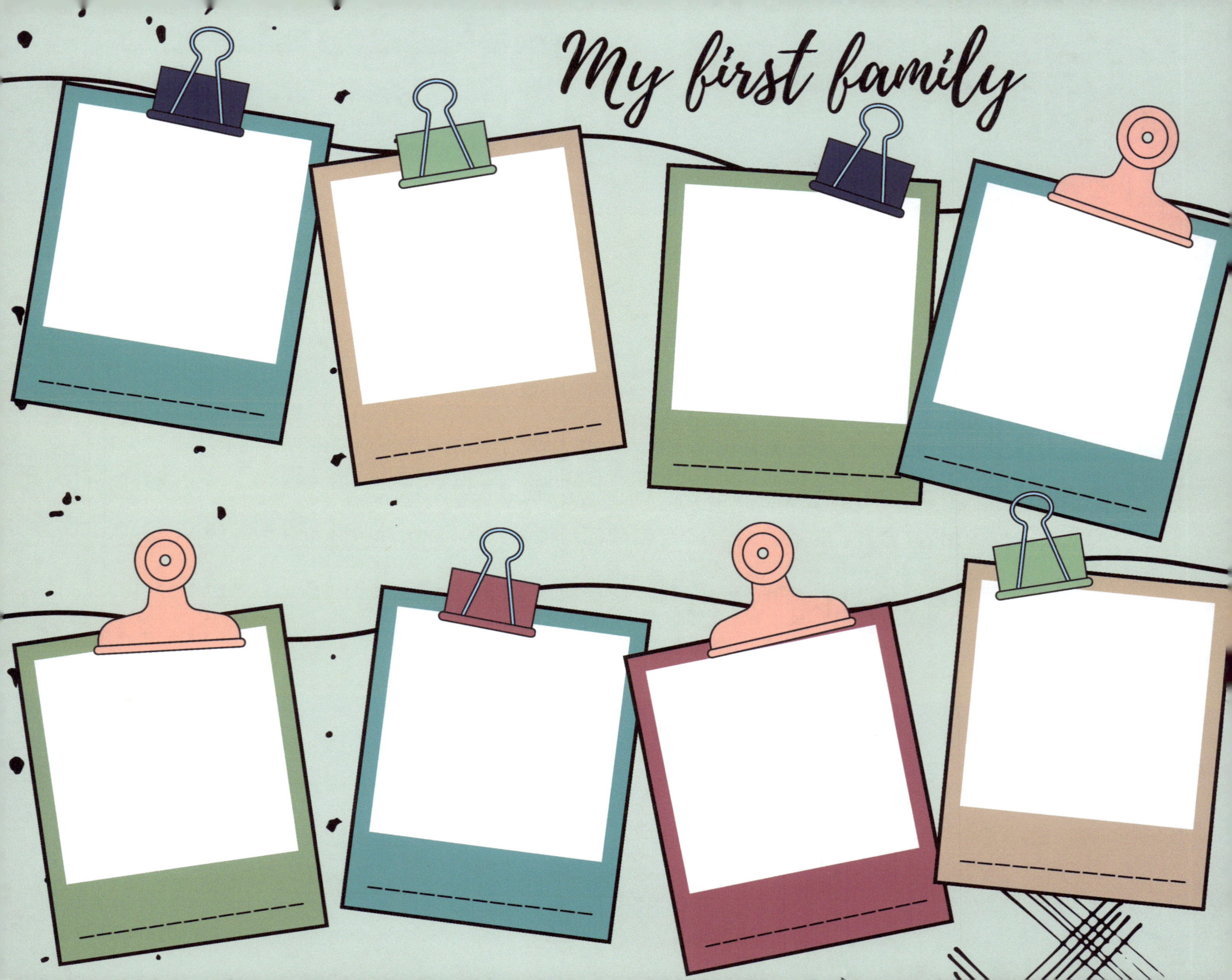

My first family

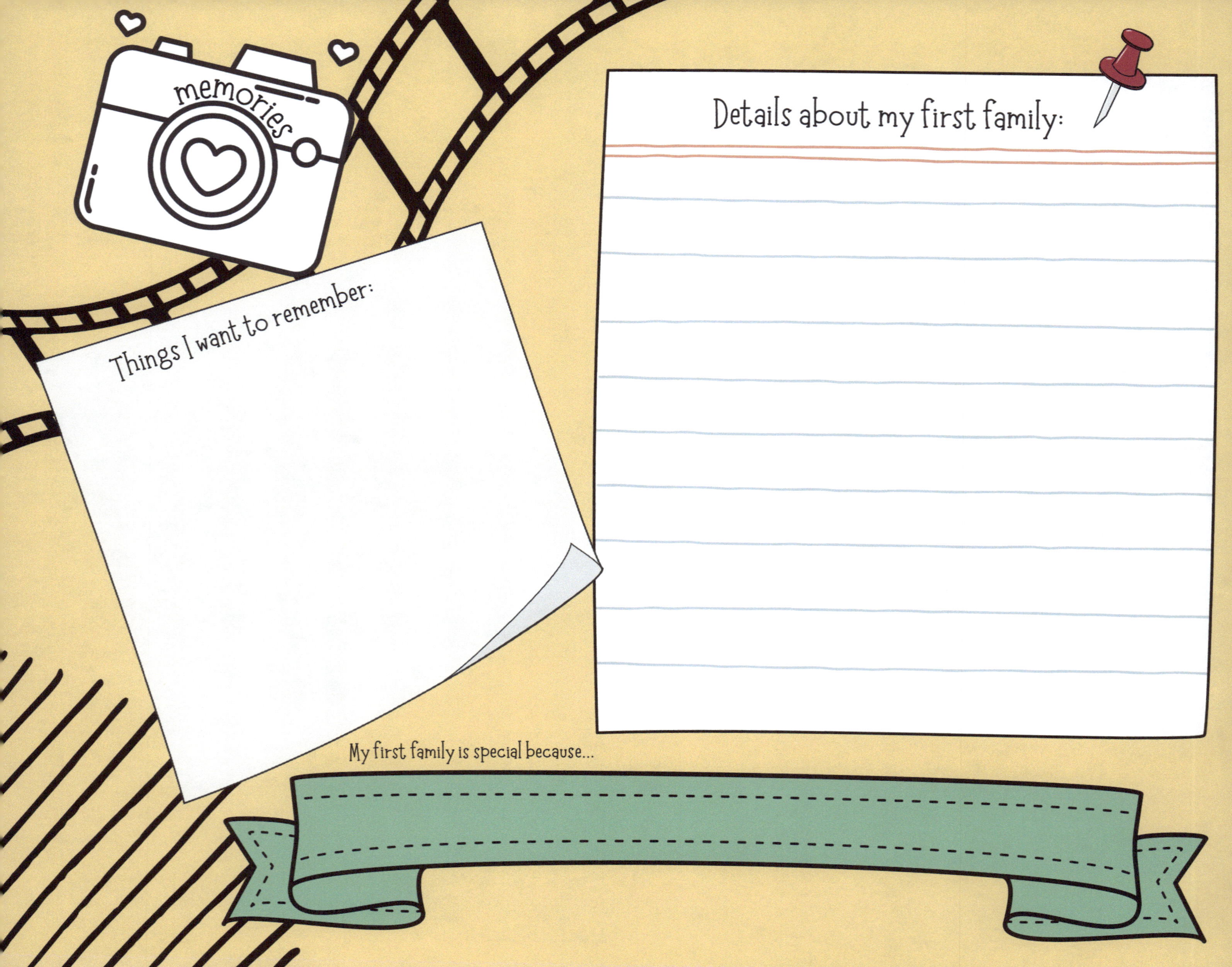
memories
Details about my first family:
Things I want to remember:
My first family is special because...

Things I want to tell my first family:
XOXO
XOXO
Traits I inherited from my first family:
♡ My prayer for my first family:

You made all the delicate, inner parts of my body
and knit me together in my mother's womb.
Thank you for making me so wonderfully complex!
Your workmanship is marvelous—how well I know it.
You watched me as I was being formed in utter seclusion,
as I was woven together in the dark of the womb.
Psalm 139:13-15

God designed you and formed you as you grew inside of your first mom. How can you thank God for the way He made you?
My JOURNAL
Attach a photo here.
God made me!
Attach a photo here.
wonderfully made
God, thank you for:

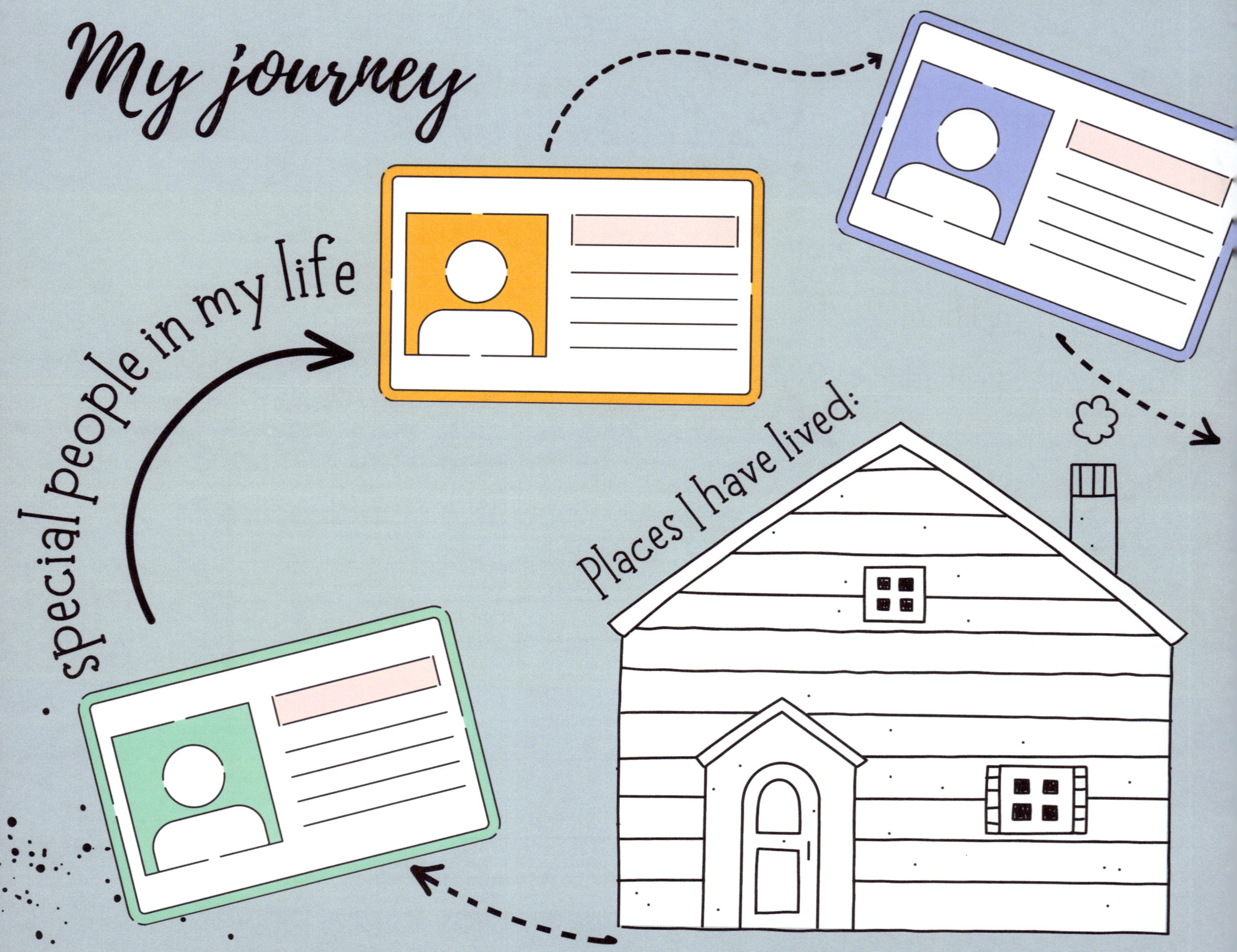

My journey
special people in my life
Places I have lived:

Memorable moments
Important life events:
Milestones & Accomplishments

You see me when I travel
and when I rest at home.
You know everything I do...
You go before me and follow me.
You place your hand of blessing on my head...
You saw me before I was born.
Every day of my life was recorded in your book.
Every moment was laid out
before a single day had passed.
Psalm 139:3,5,16

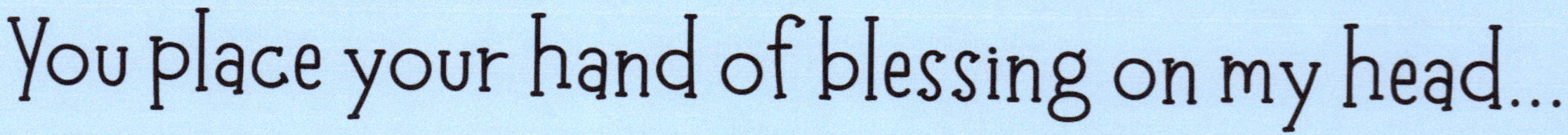

God has a plan for your life.
He knows where you have been
and where you are headed.
When you are unsure
about the road ahead,
He will guide you.
And best of all, He promises
to walk with you all along the way.
How do you need God's guidance today?
My
JOURNAL
God, please help me through...
God has a plan for...

My Adoption Day
The day I was adopted...
People who were there:

What I remember:

Encouraging Notes and Quotes

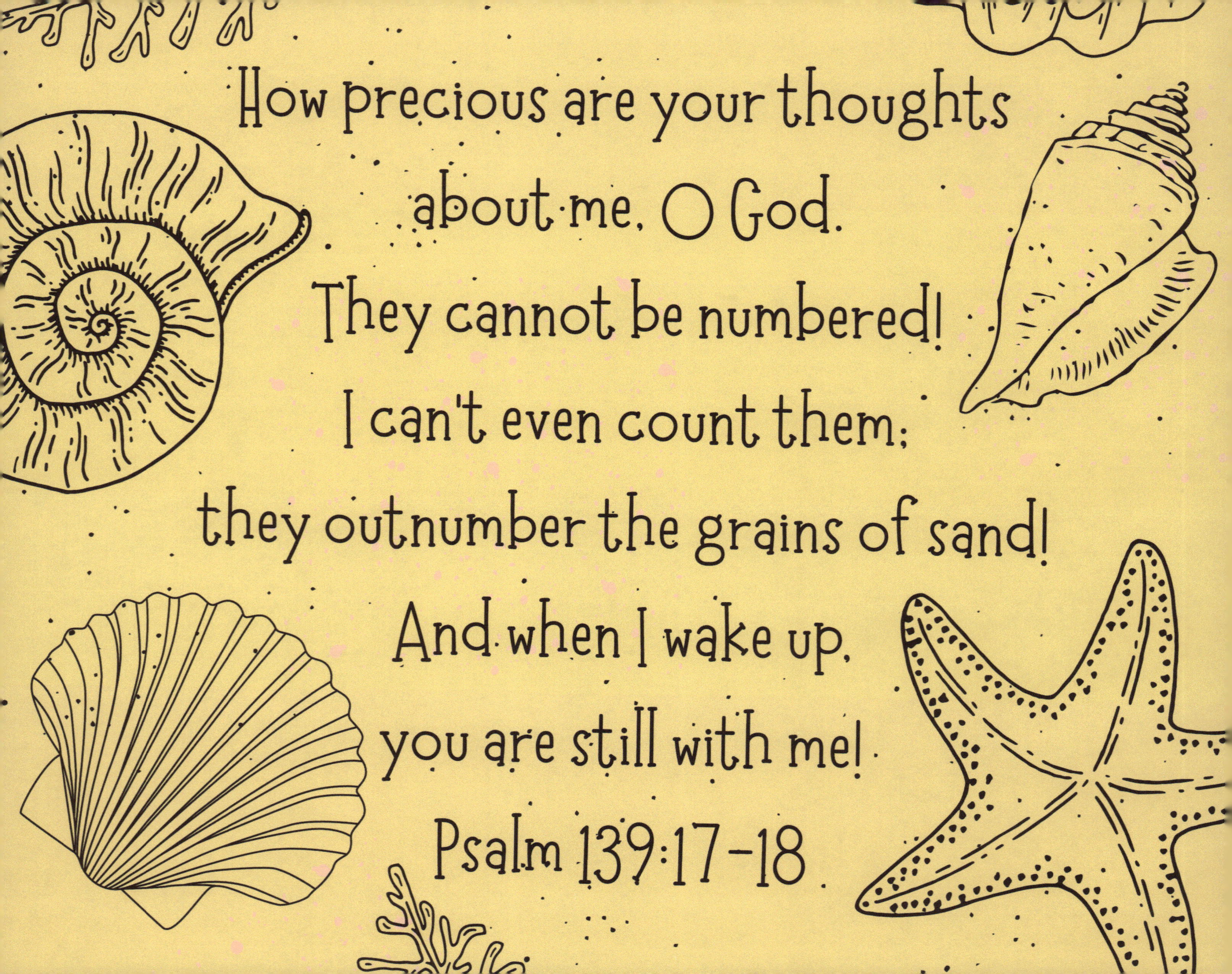

How precious are your thoughts
about me, O God.
They cannot be numbered!
I can't even count them;
they outnumber the grains of sand!
And when I wake up,
you are still with me!
Psalm 139:17-18

God thinks about you
in countless ways;
even when you are
not thinking about Him.

**He notices you
and cares about you!**

How does that truth impact you?

My forever family

Family activities
A note to my family:
Facts about my forever family:

Something special about my family:
Memories
My prayer for my forever family:
My favorite thing to do with my family is...
S.
B.
A.

I can never escape from your Spirit!
I can never get away from your presence!
If I go up to heaven, you are there;
if I go down to the grave, you are there.
If I ride the wings of the morning,
if I dwell by the farthest oceans,
even there your hand will guide me,
and your strength will support me.
Psalm 139: 7-10

Your journey of life may have some unexpected turns along the way, but God promises to guide you and support you no matter where you go. How does this truth help you as you look at the past and the future?

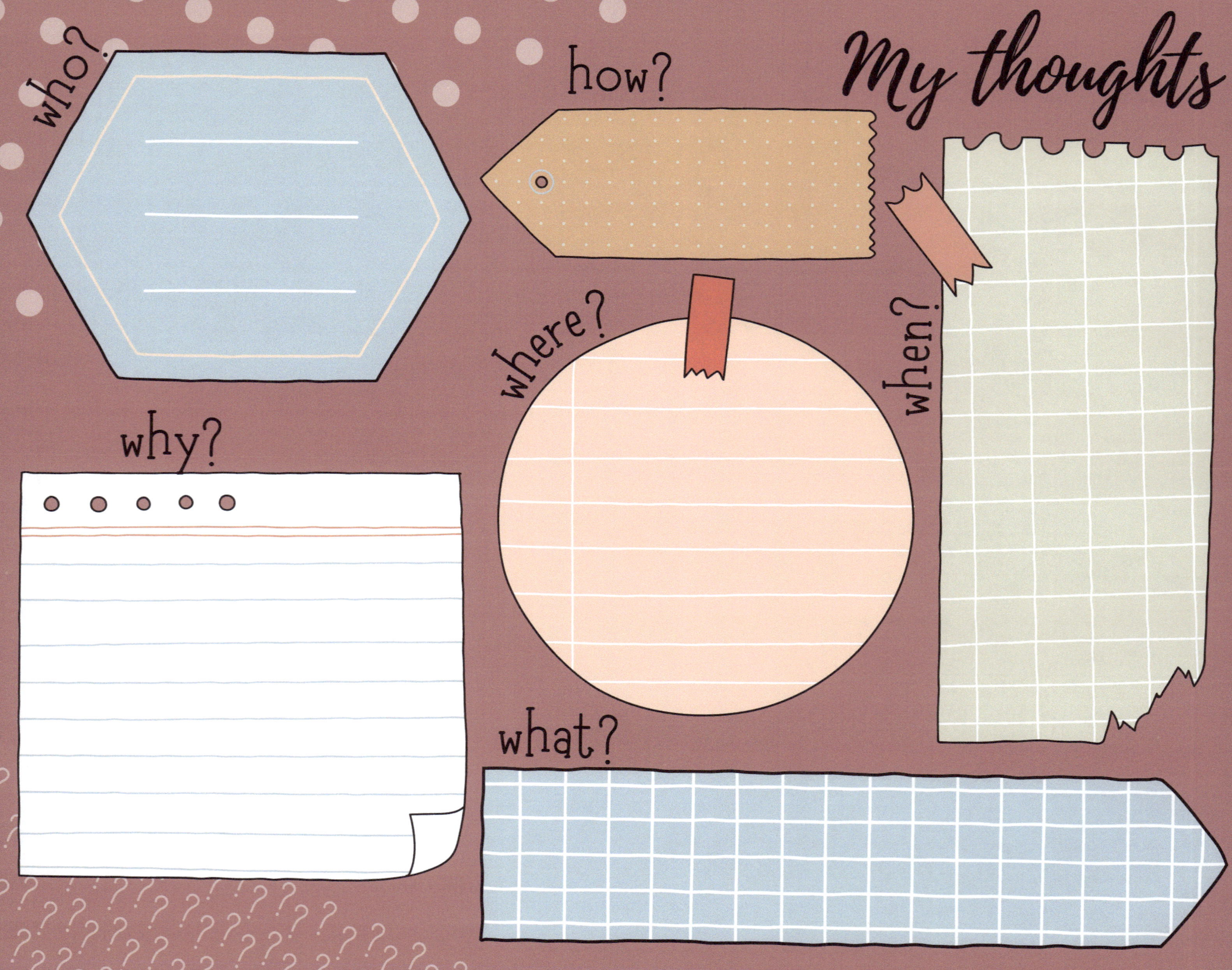

who?
how?
My thoughts
where?
when?
why?
what?

excited
sad
hopeful
thankful
angry
worried
confused

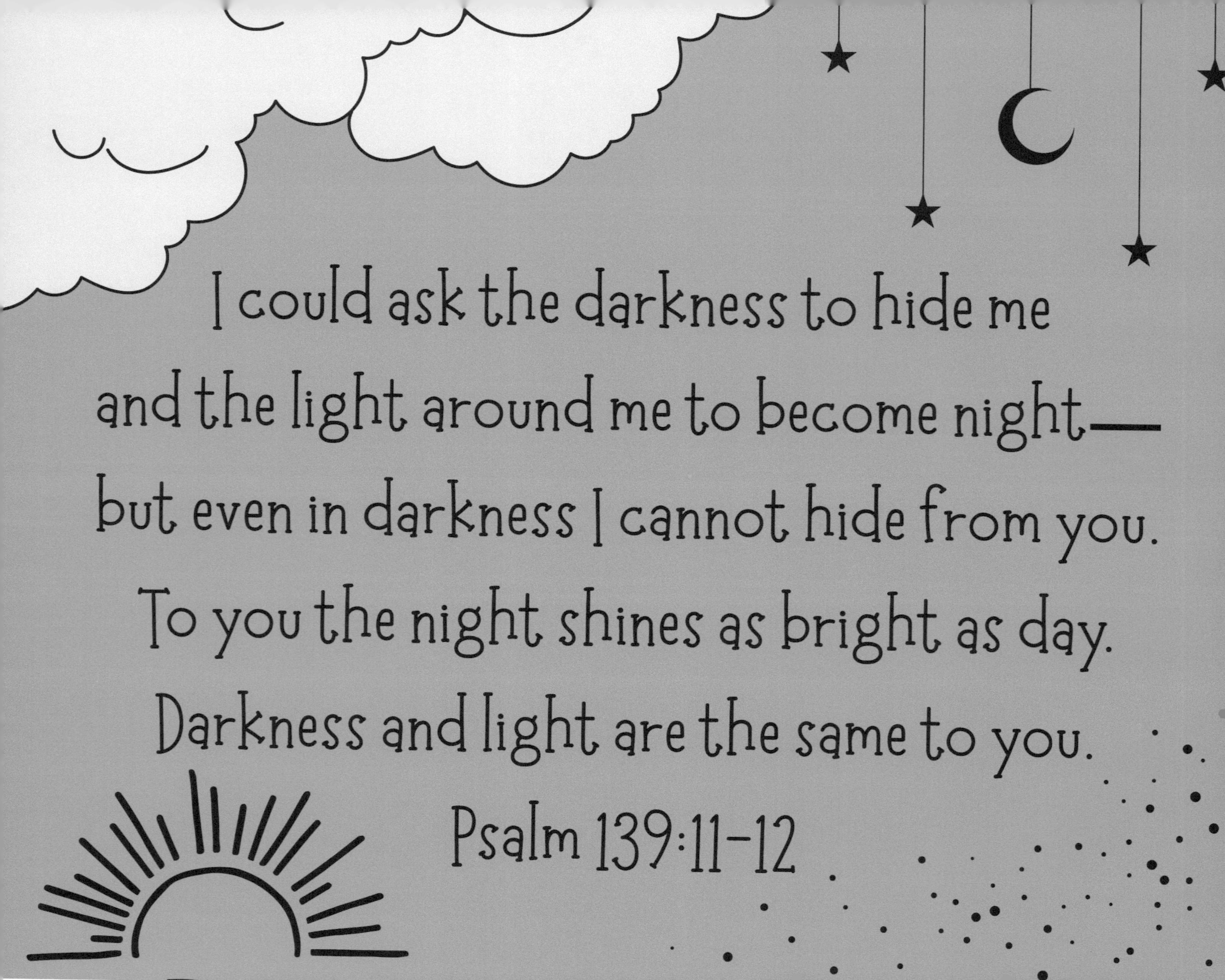
I could ask the darkness to hide me
and the light around me to become night—
but even in darkness I cannot hide from you.
To you the night shines as bright as day.
Darkness and light are the same to you.
Psalm 139:11–12

My JOURNAL

You can share your thoughts and feelings with God (even the thoughts you keep hidden in the darkness). God created your emotions. He knows your thoughts. and He is always ready to listen to your prayers.

What would you like to tell God about today?

My dreams for the future
Someday...
prayers
plans
hopes

travel
pets
home
family
job
goals
ministry

Search me, O God, and know my heart;
test me and know my anxious thoughts.
Point out anything in me that offends you,
and lead me along the path of everlasting life.
Psalm 139:23-24

Things in life are changing all of the time, but sometimes change can be a good thing. **God gradually changes you to be more like Him** as you walk along His path to eternal life. How is God working in you and changing you lately?

CAN I TRUST GOD?

"Who is God, and how do I know if I can trust Him?"

We usually don't trust people we don't know. Trusting people means that we feel safe with them, and we know they will do what they say they will do. Sometimes, even people we know let us down. Has a friend ever lied to you? Has someone close to you made you feel unsafe or left you alone? You may think that there's no one in the whole world you can trust. But, if you take some time to get to know God more, you will find that He is the best person to trust. "Fearing people is a dangerous trap, but trusting the LORD means safety." (Proverbs 29:25)

God is a Spirit. God is very different than us. He is invisible. Sometimes things that are new and different are scary. But it is actually a very good thing that God is not like us. He thinks differently than we do, and He can do things we can't do. **God is eternal.** That means that God has always been alive and always will be. A thousand years before you were born, God was there, and a billion years in the future, God will *still* be there. "All honor and glory to God forever and ever! He is the eternal King, the unseen one who never dies; he alone is God. Amen." (1 Timothy 1:17) **God is all-powerful.** He can do anything! He can make a storm stop. He can make something out of nothing. He can even hear your thoughts. "How great is our Lord! His power is absolute! His understanding is beyond comprehension!" (Psalm 147:5) A powerful person might make us feel afraid, like an evil villain in a movie. But here is the good news: **God is always good.** There is no evil in Him at all; not one little bit. Whatever He does is always the best and most loving decision He could ever make. When **God created the world**, He said that everything He made was good. But now, there are a lot of bad things in this world, right? Sometimes we get hurt or sick. Things get broken or lost. People can be selfish or unkind. What happened to God's good creation? Well, people chose to follow their own plan instead of God's plan. If God's plan is always best and good, then any other plan must be a bad plan. Choosing to go against God's plan is disobeying God, and that is called sin. Sin brought death and pain into the world, because people with bad plans do bad things. They hurt others and themselves. But this sin that spread over the whole world did not spread to God, because God is righteous. That means that **God always does what is right.** "The LORD is good and does what is right; he shows the proper path to those who go astray." (Psalm 25:8) God's righteousness also means that He must punish sin. "But the LORD of Heaven's Armies will be exalted by his justice. The holiness of God will be displayed by his righteousness." (Isaiah 5:16) Because **God is Holy**, there is no sin in Him, and people who choose to sin must be separated from Him. **God is the Perfect Judge.** If a judge doesn't follow the law and punish those who disobey the law, then he is *not* a good judge. "God alone, who gave the law, is the Judge. He alone has the power to save or to destroy." (James 4:12) God said that the punishment for sin is death; people must not be able to hurt others and themselves forever! When someone dies, their body stops working, but their soul lives on forever. Your soul is the part of you that makes you think, feel, and choose; it's the real you. After death, those who have sinned must be separated from God forever in a place called Hell. But that is not what God wants for the people He created, because **God loves everyone perfectly.** "[God] wants all people to be saved and to come to a knowledge of the truth." (1 Timothy 2:4) He loves us so much that He already had a plan in place to save us from sin and separation from Him. His Son Jesus chose to come to Earth as a human and rescue us.

Jesus is God, so He never sinned, even while He lived in a world full of sin. If Jesus never sinned, then He didn't deserve to die, right? But He *chose* to die in our place. He took the punishment that *we* deserved. That took a lot of love, for Him to choose to be punished for something He didn't do. But He did not stay dead! God is more powerful than death! After three days, Jesus resurrected; that means He brought Himself back to life again! Those who ask Him to save them will also live again. Jesus said, "I give them eternal life, and they will never perish. No one can snatch them away from me, for my Father has given them to me, and he is more powerful than anyone else. No one can snatch them from the Father's hand. The Father and I are one." (John 10:28-30) God promised that all who accept Jesus as their Savior and Lord will not be separated from God, but will live forever with Him. And we know this will happen because **God always keeps His promises.** There has never been a time, or ever will be a time, when God won't do what He said He would. "For Jesus Christ, the Son of God, does not waver between 'Yes' and 'No'...he always does what he says." (2 Corinthians 1:19) **God never lies**, because He is the Truth, and every word He speaks is true. "This truth gives them confidence that they have eternal life, which God—who does not lie—promised them before the world began." (Titus 1:2) Nothing can stop Him from keeping His promises, because He can do anything! "O Sovereign LORD! You made the heavens and earth by your strong hand and powerful arm. Nothing is too hard for you!" (Jeremiah 32:17) God doesn't go on vacation or move away; **God is always with us.** Jesus said, "And be sure of this: I am with you always, even to the end of the age." (Matthew 28:20) **God never gets tired**; He doesn't get sick or fall asleep. "Have you never heard? Have you never understood? The LORD is the everlasting God, the Creator of all the earth. He never grows weak or weary. No one can measure the depths of his understanding." (Isaiah 40:28) So there is never a time when we want to talk to God and He's not there. He's not too busy for us, because **God cares about us!** "Give all your worries and cares to God, for he cares about you." (1 Peter 5:7)

Ok, so we know God a little better now than we did before, but what if God is different tomorrow? One of the most comforting things we can know about God is that **God never changes.** Everything around us might be changing all the time: the weather, our feelings, even our friends and family. But God will always be the same, no matter what happens in our world. "God is not a man, so he does not lie. He is not human, so he does not change his mind. Has he ever spoken and failed to act? Has he ever promised and not carried it through?" (Numbers 23:19) The answer is, "No!" And that means, no matter what, we can trust God!

"I pray that God, the source of hope, will fill you completely with joy and peace because you trust in him.

Then you will overflow with confident hope through the power of the Holy Spirit." (Romans 15:13)

OUR PROBLEM: WE ALL SIN BY DISOBEYING GOD'S RULES.

"...All people...are under the power of sin. As the Scriptures say, 'No one is righteous—not even one. No one is truly wise; no one is seeking God. All have turned away; all have become useless. No one does good, not a single one.'" (Romans 3:9-12) "For everyone has sinned; we all fall short of God's glorious standard." (Romans 3:23)

THE PUNISHMENT: SIN BRINGS FOREVER DEATH AND SEPARATION FROM GOD.

"...Sin ruled over all people and brought them to death..." (Romans 5:21) "For the wages of sin is death..." (Romans 6:23)

GOD'S PRESENT: JESUS DIED ON THE CROSS AND TOOK THE PUNISHMENT WE DESERVED!

"When we were utterly helpless, Christ came at just the right time and died for us sinners. Now, most people would not be willing to die for an upright person, though someone might perhaps be willing to die for a person who is especially good. But God showed his great love for us by sending Christ to die for us while we were still sinners. And since we have been made right in God's sight by the blood of Christ, he will certainly save us from God's condemnation. For since our friendship with God was restored by the death of his Son while we were still his enemies, we will certainly be saved through the life of his Son." (Romans 5:6-10)

PARADISE: WE CAN LIVE FOREVER WITH GOD!

"Yet God, in his grace, freely makes us right in his sight. He did this through Christ Jesus when he freed us from the penalty for our sins. For God presented Jesus as the sacrifice for sin. People are made right with God when they believe that Jesus sacrificed his life, shedding his blood." (Romans 3:24-25) "For the wages of sin is death, but the free gift of God is eternal life through Christ Jesus our Lord." (Romans 6:23) "When people work, their wages are not a gift, but something they have earned. But people are counted as righteous, not because of their work, but because of their faith in God who forgives sinners." (Romans 4:4-5) "So just as sin ruled over all people and brought them to death, now God's wonderful grace rules instead, giving us right standing with God and resulting in eternal life through Jesus Christ our Lord." (Romans 5:21)

IT'S PERSONAL: WE CAN BELIEVE IN JESUS' POWER OVER DEATH AND CALL HIM OUR LORD!

"We are made right with God by placing our faith in Jesus Christ. And this is true for everyone who believes, no matter who we are." (Romans 3:22) "If you openly declare that Jesus is Lord and believe in your heart that God raised him from the dead, you will be saved. For it is by believing in your heart that you are made right with God, and it is by openly declaring your faith that you are saved... For 'Everyone who calls on the name of the LORD will be saved.'" (Romans 10:9-10, 13) "So now we can rejoice in our wonderful new relationship with God because our Lord Jesus Christ has made us friends of God." (Romans 5:11)

IT'S PERMANENT: WE ARE GOD'S CHILDREN FOREVER!

"So you have not received a spirit that makes you fearful slaves. Instead, you received God's Spirit when he adopted you as his own children. Now we call him, 'Abba, Father.' For his Spirit joins with our spirit to affirm that we are God's children." (Romans 8:15-16) "No power in the sky above or in the earth below—indeed, nothing in all creation will ever be able to separate us from the love of God that is revealed in Christ Jesus our Lord." (Romans 8:39)